ABBA

easy playalong *for* violin

WISE PUBLICATIONS
London/New York/Paris/Sydney/Copenhagen/Madrid/Tokyo

Exclusive Distributors:
Music Sales Limited
14-15 Berners Street,
London W1T 3LJ, UK.

Music Sales Pty Limited
20 Resolution Drive,
Caringbah, NSW 2229,
Australia.

Order No. AM971003
ISBN 0-7119-8933-8
This book © Copyright 2001 by Wise Publications.

Music arranged by CN Productions Ltd.
Music processed by Enigma Music Production Services.
Cover photography courtesy George Taylor.
Printed in the United Kingdom by
Printwise (Haverhill) Limited, Haverhill, Suffolk.

CD Engineered by Arthur Dick.
Instrumental solos by Dermot Crehan.

Your Guarantee of Quality:
As publishers, we strive to produce every book to
the highest commercial standards.
The music has been freshly engraved and the book
has been carefully designed to minimise awkward page
turns and to make playing from it a real pleasure.
Particular care has been given to specifying acid-free,
neutral-sized paper made from pulps which have not
been elemental chlorine bleached.
This pulp is from farmed sustainable forests and
was produced with special regard for the environment.
Throughout, the printing and binding have been planned
to ensure a sturdy, attractive publication which should
give years of enjoyment.
If your copy fails to meet our high standards,
please inform us and we will gladly replace it.

www.musicsales.com

CHIQUITITA

Words & Music by Benny Andersson & Björn Ulvaeus

20
how the heart - aches come and they go and the scars they're leav - ing.

22
You'll be danc - ing once a - gain__ and the pain will end, you will have no

25
time for griev - ing.__ Chi - qui - ti - ta, you and I cry,

28
but the sun is still in the sky and shin - in' a - bove you,__

30
let me hear_ you sing once more, like you did be - fore, sing a new song,

33
1:36
Chi - qui - ti - ta.__ Try once more like you did be -

36
- fore, sing a new song, Chi - qui - ti - ta.__ Try once

39
rall.
more like you did be - fore, sing a new song, Chi - qui - ti - ta.__

7

DANCING QUEEN

Words & Music by Benny Andersson, Björn Ulvaeus & Stig Anderson

Moderate rock

You can dance,_ you can jive,_____ hav - ing the time of your life, see that girl,_ watch that scene,_ dig - gin' the danc - ing queen._

Fri - day night and the lights are low,___ look - ing out for a place to go._ Where they play the right mu - sic, get - ting in the swing, you come to look for a king, a - ny - bo - dy could be that guy,_ night is young and the mu - sic's high, with a bit of rock mu - sic,

9

FERNANDO

Words & Music by Benny Andersson, Björn Ulvaeus & Stig Anderson

I HAVE A DREAM

Words & Music by Benny Andersson & Björn Ulvaeus

KNOWING ME, KNOWING YOU

Words & Music by Benny Andersson, Björn Ulvaeus & Stig Anderson

Break-ing up is ne-ver ea-sy I know but I have to go. Know-ing

me, know-ing you_ its the best___ I can do.

Instrumental

Know-ing me, know-ing

you, there is no-thing we can do.___ Know-ing me, know-ing

you, we just have to face it this time_ we're through.

Break-ing up is nev-er ea-sy I know but I have to go. Know-ing

me, know-ing you,_ its the best___ I can do.

LAY ALL YOUR LOVE ON ME

Words & Music by Benny Andersson & Björn Ulvaeus

I was-n't jea-lous be-fore we met,

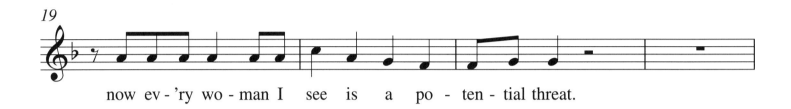

now ev-'ry wo-man I see is a po-ten-tial threat.

And I'm po-sess-ive it is-n't nice, you've heard me say-ing that

smo-king was my on-ly vice. But now it is-n't true,

now ev-'ry-thing is new, and all I've learned_ has

ov-er-turned_ I beg of you:_____

MAMMA MIA

Words & Music by Benny Andersson, Björn Ulvaeus & Stig Anderson

THE NAME OF THE GAME

Words & Music by Benny Andersson, Björn Ulvaeus & Stig Anderson

S.O.S.

Words & Music by Benny Andersson, Björn Ulvaeus & Stig Anderson

SUPER TROUPER

Words & Music by Benny Andersson & Björn Ulvaeus

MONEY, MONEY, MONEY

Words & Music by Benny Andersson & Björn Ulvaeus

THANK YOU FOR THE MUSIC

Words & Music by Benny Andersson & Björn Ulvaeus

I'm no-thing spe-cial, in fact I'm a bit_ of a bore,_

if I tell a joke_ you've pro-bab-ly heard_ it be-fore._

But I have a tal-ent, a won-der-ful thing,_ 'cause ev-'ry-one lis-tens when

I start to sing._ I'm so grate-ful and proud,_ all I want is to sing_ it out loud._

_ So I say, thank-you for the mu-sic, the songs I'm sing-ing, thanks for all the

joy they're bring-ing. Who can live with-out it? I ask in all ho-nes-ty,_

_ what would life be,_ with-out a song_ or dance_ what are we? So I say,

thank-you for the mu-sic, for giv-ing it to me.

So I say thank-you for the mu-sic, for giv-ing it to me.

TAKE A CHANCE ON ME

Words & Music by Benny Andersson & Björn Ulvaeus

Moderately

WATERLOO

Words & Music by Benny Andersson, Björn Ulvaeus & Stig Anderson

THE WINNER TAKES IT ALL

Words & Music by Benny Andersson & Björn Ulvaeus

3/09 (169120)